STEM Junior

MATH

KINGFISHER

LONDON & NEW YORK

KINGFISHER
LONDON & NEW YORK

Text and design copyright © Toucan Books Ltd. 2020
Illustrations copyright © Simon Basher 2020
www.basherscience.com

First published 2020 in the United States by Kingfisher
120 Broadway, New York, NY 10271
Kingfisher is an imprint of Macmillan Children's Books, London
All rights reserved.

Author: Jonathan O'Callaghan
Consultant: Troy Regis
Editor: Anna Southgate
Designer: Leah Germann
Indexer: Marie Lorimer
Proofreader: Richard Beatty

Dedicated to Poppy, Theo, and Ted

Distributed in the U.S. and Canada by Macmillan,
120 Broadway, New York, NY 10271

Library of Congress Cataloging-in-Publication Data has been applied for.

ISBN: 978-0-7534-7561-4 (Hardcover)
ISBN: 978-0-7534-7557-7 (Paperback)

Kingfisher books are available for special promotions and premiums.
For details contact: Special Markets Department, Macmillan, 120 Broadway,
New York, NY 10271

For more information, please visit www.kingfisherbooks.com

Printed in China
9 8 7 6 5 4 3 2 1
1TR/0420/WKT/UG/128MA

Contents

Math-tastic!

Are you ready to step into the amazing world of math? Well, you'd better prepare yourself for a treat, because you are not going to believe how many things there are to discover! We're not just talking numbers here. This incredible place is packed with symbols and shapes and graphs and so much more.

You must know that humans have been using math for thousands of years. The figure Zero is ancient, as is Pi and its Geometry Genius pals. But don't be fooled by age. Every single character in this book is essential to life in the modern world. How else do you think your computer would work? Or your TV? How would planes stay up in the sky? Without math these things just wouldn't be possible. Why don't you find out for yourself — these colorful characters are itching to tell you all there is to know.

Zero

Infinity

Integer

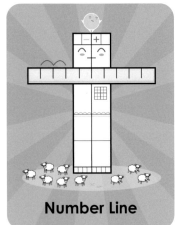

Number Line

Fraction

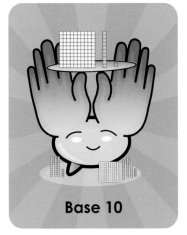

Base 10

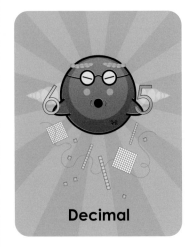

Decimal

Composite Number

Prime Number

Nimble Numbers

You probably think you know all about numbers already. So let's see . . . have you ever met Integer or Base 10 before? Hm? Sure, you've heard of Prime Number, but do you know how many digits the biggest prime has? And can you tell Fraction from Decimal? Too many questions? Let these amazing characters give you some answers. There are even some surprises in store!

Zero
★ Absolutely Nothing

THE BIG IDEA

A number that means you have nothing of something. It is found above −1 and below 1 on the number line.

Ha! See that massive hole in my middle? Well, that just about sums me up. I'm Zero, and I amount to nothing. Just see what happens if you try to add or subtract me from a number. Nothing! The number just stays the same.

Some say I'm low, but who can blame me, when they call me names such as *zip*, *zilch*, and *nada*? I'm not even the lowest — there are millions of **negative** numbers below me! Plus, my pal Base 10 would be powerless without me. How else could it make all those 10s, 100s, and 1,000s?

⊙ A number multiplied by zero is always zero: 5 × 0 = 0

⊙ Dividing by zero makes a calculator say ERROR, as it is not possible

⊙ Bees can recognize when there is nothing compared to something

SAY WHAT?

Negative: Any number below zero is negative. A negative number is written using a negative sign: −5. A number above zero is positive.

✳ ANCIENT ZEROES ✳

Zero was first used 5,000 years ago in a place called Mesopotamia — that's southern Iraq today. The Sumerian people who lived there came up with a number system and used a symbol to show when they had nothing.

Infinity

★ Endless Oddity

THE BIG IDEA

The idea that numbers go on and on and on, without end, in both directions above and below zero.

Imagine doing nothing but counting numbers for your entire life. How high would you get? Well, you'd reach a pretty big number, but you'd never get near me! I'm Infinity, and I'm bigger than the biggest number you can imagine (and smaller than the smallest).

I'm so weirdly endless that in medieval times people used to show me as a snake biting its tail. The truth is, I'm not a number in the sense that 1, 2, and 3 are numbers. You can't use me to measure things or to add up. I'm more of a distant number cousin, but I like to keep that to myself!

- ◉ The ancient Greeks first understood infinity about 2,000 years ago

- ◉ Infinity can be positive and negative

SAY WHAT?

Lemniscate: The name given to infinity's "sideways eight" looped symbol (∞).

✳ MATH LEGEND ✳

John Wallis was an English mathematician. In 1655, he published a book that explained how infinity works. He was the first person to use the **lemniscate** that we still use to represent infinity.

Integer

★ Wholesome Sort

THE BIG IDEA

Any whole number that is higher or lower than zero, including zero itself.

Nimble Numbers don't come more "wholesome" than me. My name is Integer, and I'm any complete number that you can think of, negative or positive. The **natural numbers** 1, 2, 3, and so on, are all integers, but so are –1, –2, –3 . . . ! Even zero is in my gang.

I'm mostly used for counting real-life things — you know, stuff like books, marbles, and friends. But I don't hang out with Fraction or Decimal. No way! They are not complete, and they are not in my club. Well, when did you ever hear of half a baseball bat or see 2.7 kites in the sky?

◉ All whole numbers are integers, no matter how high or low

◉ Integers can be added, subtracted, multiplied, and divided

⚡ SAY WHAT? ⚡

Natural numbers: Also called the counting numbers, these are any whole numbers above (but not including) zero.

✳ APPLYING SCIENCE ✳

Computers, smartphones, and tablet PCs all use integers every day. They use "binary" numbers, which are just 1s and 0s to you and me. The numbers help make sure that all your games and videos run smoothly!

Number Line

★ Straight Talker

THE BIG IDEA

A way of showing how much space there is between numbers on a straight line. Markers are used to place each new number.

A farmer has nine sheep, but three run away. How many are left? One hen on the farm lays seven eggs, and another lays six. How many eggs in total? Adding and subtracting can be tricky, right? But not with me helping out. I'm Number Line — a line marked with numbers!

My friend Zero sits at my center, with positive numbers heading to the right and negative numbers to the left. Take the the first number of a **sum** as your starting point and count up my line for addition and down for subtraction. For those eggs, it means starting at 7 and counting 6 to the right: 8, 9, 10, 11, 12, 13!

- Number lines can be used for negative and positive numbers

- Two number lines at right angles can form a graph

 SAY WHAT?

Sum: Adding any two or more numbers together is called finding a sum: 1 plus 1 creates a sum, and so does 2 plus 5 plus 3 plus 1.

 DO IT YOURSELF

Make your own number line. Use a ruler and a pencil to draw a straight line on a sheet of paper. Start with 0 and write out the numbers to 10, spacing your numbers evenly along its length. Now give yourself some sums to find!

Fraction

★ Number Splitter

THE BIG IDEA

One way to represent the parts that make up a whole number.

What happens when you cut a round cake into six equal wedges? You get me, Fraction! Each wedge is just one part of the whole: one-sixth. Hovering somewhere between Zero and the number 1, I'm written like this: $\frac{1}{6}$. My top number is called the **numerator** and my bottom number is called the **denominator**.

Wholesome Integer thinks I'm sad, because I'm broken, but I think I look fantastic. In any case, you need not-whole numbers like me. How else can you say how much cake is left after a naughty mouse has come along and nibbled a wedge away?

- A "proper" fraction is less than 1 — for example, $\frac{7}{8}$

- An "improper" fraction is more than 1 — for example, $\frac{12}{8}$

- There are an infinite number of fractions between 0 and 1

SAY WHAT?

Numerator: tells you how many parts of the whole you have.

Denominator: tells you how many parts make the whole.

APPLYING SCIENCE

Fractions can be simplified. Sharing your cake equally among three people means each has $\frac{2}{6}$ of the cake, which can also be written $\frac{1}{3}$. Sharing the cake between two of you means each has $\frac{3}{6}$ or $\frac{1}{2}$.

Base 10

★ Group Power

Hi, I'm Base 10, a most fabulous counting system. Of course, you can count using the tips of your fingers (and thumbs), but you'll find me useful when working with numbers bigger than 20.

I use my pal Zero and sets of ten **units** to write numbers in columns of 1s, 10s, 100s, 1,000s, and so on. In any column, the value of the number is ten times that of the number to its right. Don't panic! It's not tricky. You see, 34 just means three tens, and four ones: thirty-four! A new column to the left, 134, gives one hundred, three tens and four ones: one hundred thirty-four! See how easy it is?

◉ Base 10 was used by the ancient Egyptians about 5,000 years ago

◉ The metric system is based on multiples of 10

◉ This system is also known as the place-value system

SAY WHAT?

Unit: A single group of something. Unit can also mean "1."

MENTAL MATH

See if you can use Base 10 to count some huge numbers. Here are a few to try. Figure out how many 1,000s, 100s, 10s, and 1s are in these numbers: 2,153 and 4,286. What about 68,947?

That last one has sixty-eight thousands, nine hundreds, four tens, and seven ones: sixty-eight thousand, nine hundred forty-seven.

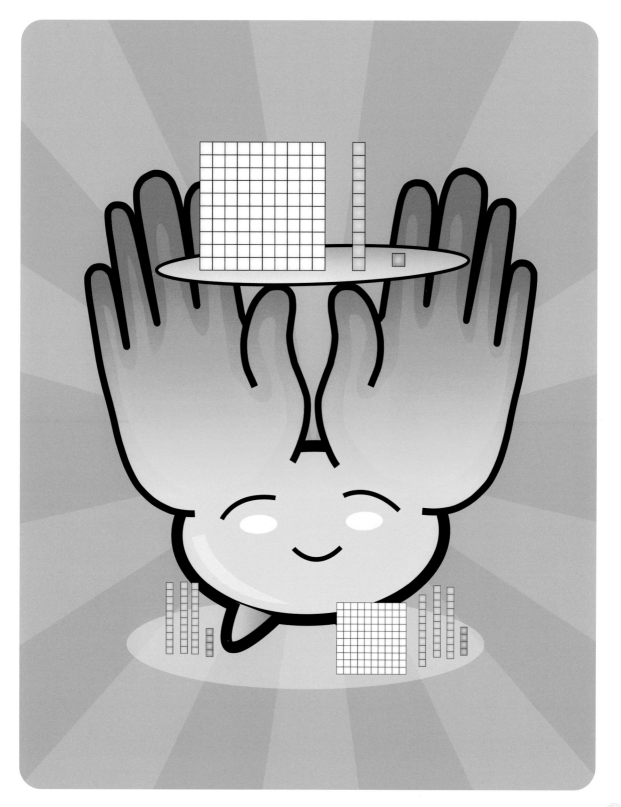

Decimal

★ Mega Splitter

THE BIG IDEA

A form of not-whole number that is expressed using a dot.
The dot is called a decimal point or a radix point.

You've met my buddy Fraction? Well, I'm Decimal, and I involve not-whole numbers, too. While Fraction has a top and a bottom, I use a decimal-digit "string." My perfect little dot marks the exact spot where a whole number ends and a not-whole number begins.

I work in multiples of ten, and the numbers to the right of my dot are "tenths" of a whole. This means $6\frac{1}{2}$ becomes 6.5. I'm precise, but not always neat! In my world, two wedges of that cake the mouse ate make 0.66666666, with the 6s **recurring**.

- ◉ Chinese mathematicians were using decimals about 2,400 years ago

- ◉ The Latin word *decimus* means "tenth" and is the origin of "decimal"

- ◉ Decimal numbers go to infinity in both directions

⚡ SAY WHAT? ⚡

Recurring: A decimal number that repeats the same sequence without end, as in 1.457457457. . . Never-ending decimal numbers that have no repeat sequence are irrational numbers.

✳ MENTAL MATH ✳

Can you turn fractions into decimals? If $6\frac{1}{10}$ is 6.1, how would you write $6\frac{7}{10}$? You can think about numbers such as 4.25 as four and twenty-five hundredths. How would you read 4.27?

The answer is four and twenty-seven hundredths.

Composite Number

★ End Product

THE BIG IDEA

A whole number that has more than two factors. Factors are numbers you can multiply together to get another number.

Hi, I'm Composite Number, and I'm made of three or more factors. Let me explain. All numbers are the **product** of "factor pairs." The number 10 has two sets of factor pairs: 1 times 10 and 2 times 5. You can see that 10 has four factors: 1, 2, 5, and 10. That makes it one of me.

Take note! The number 9 also has two factor pairs: 1 times 9 and 3 times 3. It is also composite, but it only has *three* factors: 1, 3, and 9. That's because you only list each factor once. And remember this: all composite numbers and their factors are whole numbers, but not all whole numbers are composite!

- ◉ Composite numbers always have three or more factors; the factors always include 1 and the composite number itself

- ◉ 840 has 32 factors, the most of any whole number up to 1,000

SAY WHAT?

Product: The name given to the result when you multiply numbers together: 10 is the product of 2 × 5.

MENTAL MATH

You also use factors when dividing. Dividing the number 24, you can use 2 as one factor because it is even. Now find the missing pair number that multiplies to make 24. The answer is 12. Try the number 15. If one factor in a pair is 5, what is the other one?

The answer is 3.

Prime Number
★ Tough Nut

THE BIG IDEA

A number that can be divided evenly *only* by 1 and itself. Every prime number has exactly two factors.

A hard nut to crack, I'm Prime Number. I only ever have two factors, and they are always the number 1 and myself.

My friend Composite Number gets everywhere, but compared to that boaster, I'm super rare. Ha! There are only 25 prime numbers between 1 and 100, and only 168 prime numbers between 1 and 1,000! Although I exist all the way into infinity, not even the brainiest math geeks can figure out how to find me. Good luck looking, but you'll never catch me. I'm in my *prime*!

⊙ The numbers 1 and 0 don't count as being prime

⊙ 2 has only two factors (1 and itself), and is the only even prime number

⊙ No prime number greater than 5 ends in a 5

⚡ SAY WHAT? ⚡

Digit: Any whole number from zero to nine. All large numbers are made up of digits. The digits 2, 3, 5, and 7 are prime.

＊ APPLYING SCIENCE ＊

Finding bigger and bigger prime numbers is really difficult. Scientists use super-powerful computers to look for them. The biggest prime number that we know of has more than 24 million **digits** and was discovered in 2018!

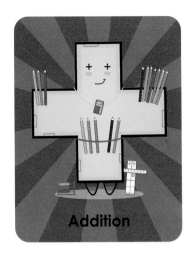

Addition

Subtraction

Multiplication

Division

Variable

Square Number

Exponent

Expression

Parentheses

Operations Team

Here's an all-singing, all-dancing crew of smooth "operators." Even the most basic kinds of math would be impossible without these guys. This is where you'll find those ancient heroes Addition, Subtraction, Multiplication, and Division. Come and meet them — and find out how they work their magic with numbers. They don't always operate alone. Sometimes they enlist a little help from Expression, Exponent, and Variable — among others — along the way.

Addition

★ Number Giver

THE BIG IDEA

A process that involves adding two or more numbers together to make a sum. A sum is the answer to an addition problem.

One of four brainy math **operations**, I'm the one that adds numbers together: Addition. Look out for my handy little symbol: +. It's called a "plus" sign, and I'll show you how it works.

You have five colored pencils, and your dad gives you another three — that's 5 + 3 = 8. If your mom gives you seven more, that's 5 + 3 + 7 = 15. You can use my friend Number Line to help you find the sums . . . or an abacus or a calculator or your fingers and toes. I'm not short of tools to help you watch those numbers grow!

⊙ "Addition" comes from the Latin *addere*, meaning "to add"

⊙ When adding numbers, it helps to start with the biggest

⊙ Adding zero to a number leaves it the same: 5 + 0 = 5

⚡ SAY WHAT? ⚡

Operation: One of four major processes used in math: addition, subtraction, multiplication, and division.

✳ MENTAL MATH ✳

Be careful when adding numbers together. If some of the numbers you're adding are negative, the sum you make could be smaller instead of bigger. For example: 5 + –3 = 2.

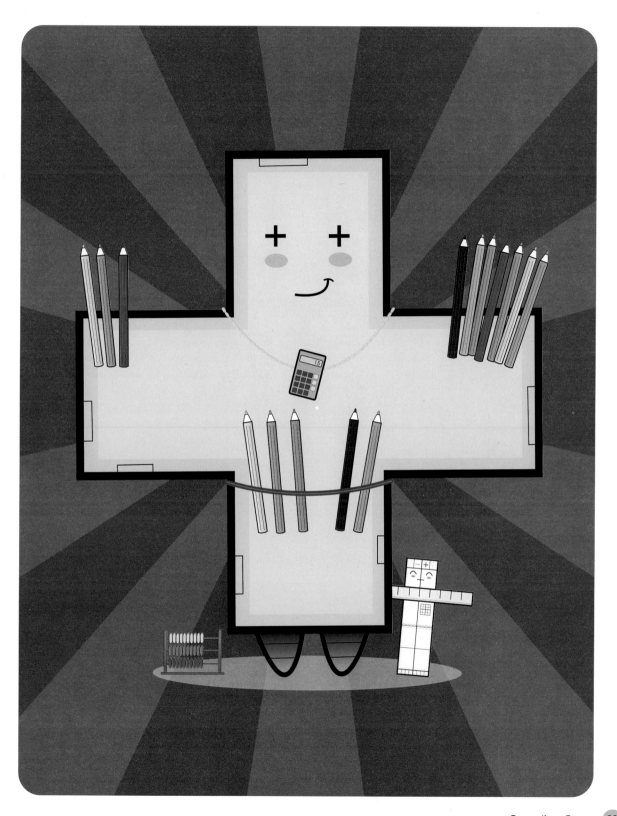

Subtraction

★ Number Taker

Don't look at me for handouts! I'm Subtraction, and I prefer to take things away. My little symbol is called a "minus" sign, and it looks like this: –. Here's how I use it. Say you have ten balloons at your birthday party, and the girl next door pops four of them. That's 10 – 4 = 6.

I happen when one number is removed from another to find the difference. I usually take a small number from a bigger one: 9 – 7 = 2. But sometimes I work the other way around, taking a big number from a smaller one to give a negative number: 7 – 9 = –2. What a meanie!

- "Subtraction" comes from Latin *subtrahere*, "to take away"

- The minus sign was first used in the 1400s

- Subtracting zero from a number leaves it the same: 5 – 0 = 5

MENTAL MATH

With big numbers, try starting from the smallest and counting the difference to the biggest. For example, try 5,432 – 3,920. Jump from 3,920 to 4,000, then 4,000 to 5,000, then 5,000 to 5,432. Add your jumps and you'll have the difference: 80 + 1,000 + 432 = 1,512

Multiplication

★ Product Pal

> ☆ **THE BIG IDEA** ☆
>
> A form of repeated addition where groups of the same size are combined together. The answer is called the product.

I make my friend Addition look super slow. Just look at my name to see why. I'm Multiplication. My *multi* basically means "many," and I use a cool symbol that looks like this: ×. It says you need to "times" the number that follows.

If you drink three glasses of milk on every school day, that's 5×3, meaning $3 + 3 + 3 + 3 + 3$, which equals 15. My product, or answer, is simply the total number from all the groups combined together. See what I mean about making Addition look sluggish?

⚡ **SAY WHAT?** ⚡

Multiplication tables: Lists that show the numbers 1 to 12 multiplied by each other. They are handy for finding products quickly.

✳ **MENTAL MATH** ✳

Sometimes you'll need to multiply two numbers that you can't easily figure out in your head, such as 23×7. Instead, think of 23 as $20 + 3$. Then multiply each of these by 7 and add the products together: $20 \times 7 + 3 \times 7$ is $140 + 21 = 161$.

- ◉ Any number multiplied by 1 remains unchanged: $7 \times 1 = 7$

- ◉ Multiples of 5 always end with the number 5 or 0

- ◉ It's weird, but $111111111 \times 111111111 = 12345678987654321$

Division

★ Fair Sharer

THE BIG IDEA

A process of splitting a larger number into equal groups of smaller numbers. The answer is called a quotient.

The last of the four math operations, I like to undo Multiplication's good work. I break down a big number into smaller ones by using a **divisor** to "split" it into even groups.

Some say I'm the toughest operation to work with, but I'm fair minded. Are you? When you have 20 pieces of candy to share among yourself and three good friends, just remember my symbol: ÷. That same-size dot above and below a dividing line means that everyone gets an equal amount. So, with those candies of yours, you'd be sure to give everybody five each, *wouldn't* you?

- The Latin word *dividere* is the origin of "divide"

- Any number divided by 1 remains unchanged: 7 ÷ 1 = 7

- Some divisions can be infinitely long if the remainder isn't precise!

⚡ SAY WHAT? ⚡

Divisor: The name given to the number doing the dividing. In 20 ÷ 5, the divisor is 5.

* MENTAL MATH *

Be careful! Not all division ends in perfect whole numbers. Sometimes you might have a "remainder," which you need to show using a fraction or a decimal. For example: 12 ÷ 5 = 2, with a remainder of 2. You can write this as $2\frac{2}{5}$ or 2.4.

Variable

★ Mystery Machine

THE BIG IDEA

A value in an **equation** that needs to be found, often with the help of an operation and other numbers.

Have you ever seen math that looks like this: $y + 7 = 9$? Well, the y is me, Variable, hiding behind a mask. Usually presented as a letter of the alphabet, I stand for a value that is not yet known.

The secret lies in the "equal" sign, because the math on either side of it must come to the same answer. You can figure it out by reversing the operations. So, if $y + 7 = 9$, then $9 - 7 = y$. Use what you already know about subtraction to find your answer, and there I am, unmasked for all to see: $y = 2$.

- The Latin word *variare* is the origin of the modern "variable"

- Variables first became popular in the 1600s

- Computers use variables for storing and using information

⚡ SAY WHAT? ⚡

Equation: A statement in which elements on either side of an equal sign are the same. For example, $1 + 2 = 3$.

✱ APPLYING SCIENCE ✱

Variables are used in equations to show that something is unknown. It is always possible to work out a variable using one or more of the four operations. Sometimes equations have more than one variable, and this can make them difficult to solve.

Square Number
★ Identical Factor

> **THE BIG IDEA**
>
> Any number that has been multiplied by itself. The products of these special multiplications are called square numbers.

Remember Composite Number with all those factors? Well, I'm the answer you get when two factors are identical — say 2 × 2 or 3 × 3. I'm written as 2^2 or 3^2. I'm Square Number, and I'm *soooo* square, I deserve a medal.

You can use my **square root** as a measurement for drawing lines. And when you draw those lines at right angles to each other, they make two sides of a *square*. And that's just the start of my clever trickery, but I'll let the Geometry Geniuses tell you more . . .

- ◉ Every square number has a pair of identical factors

- ◉ If you square an odd number, the answer is always odd

- ◉ Square an even number, and the answer is always even

⚡ **SAY WHAT?** ⚡

Square root: The number used to make a square number. For example, 5 is the square root of 25, because 5 × 5 = 25.

✳ **MATH LEGEND** ✳

There are no squares of negative numbers, because if you multiply a negative by a negative, you get a positive! This was first realized by an Indian mathematician named Mahavira in the 800s.

Exponent

★ Mega Multiplier

Hi, I'm Exponent. Multiplication thinks it's speedy, but nothing makes a number grow with less effort than I do. And Square Number? What a boaster! I put the little ^{2} in 3^2! An exponent of ^{3} means three bases multiplied together; ^{4} is four bases; and so on. Let me give you an example:

Your teacher has eight paper clips but needs more. Take the number 6. With Addition, your teacher has 8 + 6 = 14 paper clips. Multiplication gives the teacher 8 × 6 = 48 paper clips. But my 8^6 (8 × 8 × 8 × 8 × 8 × 8) offers a lifetime's supply of 262,144 paper clips!

- The number that an exponent is attached to is called a "base"

- Any number to the **power** of 0 always equals 1

- Exponents are useful for making equations shorter to write

✳ MATH LEGEND ✳

German mathematician Michael Stifel was the first person to use the word "exponent" in 1544. He realized if you multiply two of the same bases with exponents, you could add the exponents together. So $2^3 × 2^2$ is the same as 2^5.

Expression
★ Equation Maker

THE BIG IDEA

A set of numbers and symbols that combine to produce a new value — in other words, one side of an equation.

If you've ever played around with Addition, Subtraction, Multiplication, and Division, then you have been using me! I'm Expression, and I'm an essential building block in an equation that you need to solve. In the simple equation $2 + 2 = 4$, the expression is $2 + 2$. That's me.

I'm not always so basic, though. I love to use more than one operation. Take $3 + 4 - 2 + 6$. There are three operations right there! You can use each expression as a block building up to the answer: 3 plus 4 is 7; minus 2 is 5; plus 6 is 11.

⊙ There is no **equal sign** in an expression

⊙ An expression with an answer and an = sign is an equation

⊙ Using letters to represent numbers is called algebra

⚡ SAY WHAT? ⚡

Equal sign: This symbol (=) works like a balance — an expression or number on one side equals that on the other side: $4 \times 3 = 20 - 8$

✱ APPLYING SCIENCE ✱

An equation can involve several different elements. There will be one or more operations. Different letters of the alphabet can be used to show any variables. Expressions help us break down an equation, making it easier to understand.

Parentheses

★ Super Groupers

> **THE BIG IDEA**
>
> **Punctuation** that separates the expressions found in an equation, making a math problem easier to solve.

You might know us from English class, but we're useful in math too. You'll see us facing each other in an equation, making sure Expression stays in check.

We can stop you from making mistakes. Look at $2 + 6 \times 2 = x$. Is the answer 16? Or could it be 14? Allow us to step in, and all becomes clear: $2 + (6 \times 2) = x$. See now? We show you exactly which parts of an equation belong together. In this case the calculation goes $2 + 12 = 14$.

- ◉ "Parenthesis" comes from Greek *parentithenai*, "to insert"

- ◉ Complex equations might use parentheses within parentheses

- ◉ Parentheses are useful in writing to include extra information

⚡ SAY WHAT? ⚡

Punctuation: Usually, symbols that divide written words into sentences and clauses. Certain symbols, such as parentheses, are also used in math.

✳ APPLYING SCIENCE ✳

If you see parentheses in an equation, do what is inside them first. They are also used to show multiplication if next to each other. If you see $(3 + 5)(6 - 2)$, then you would first add and subtract, making $(8)(4)$, then multiply to get 32!

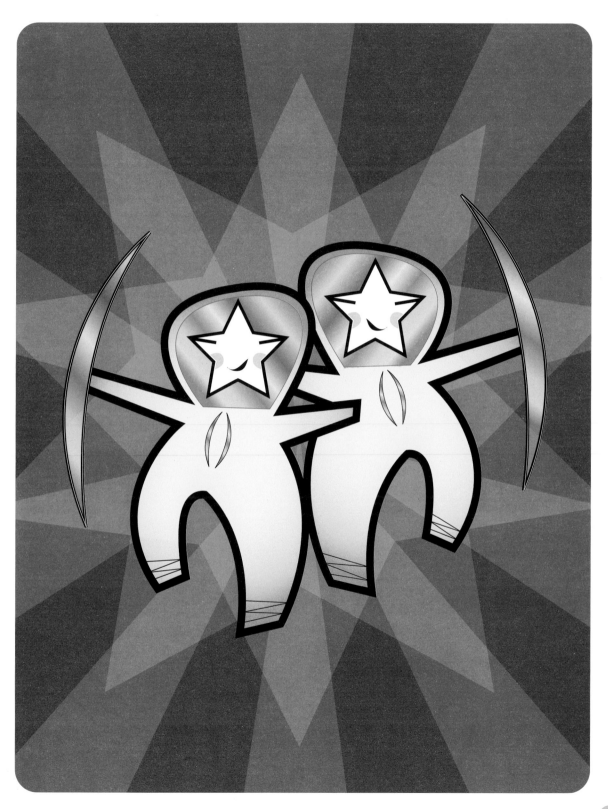

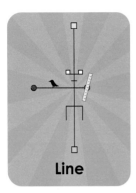

Line

Angle

Polygon

Triangle

Quadrilateral

Circle

Pi

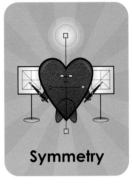

Symmetry

2-D Shape

3-D Shape

Length

Area

Volume

Geometry Geniuses

Oh look, who do we have here? Some pretty intrepid mathematicians, that's who. Almost everything you see around you has something to do with geometry, and these characters are here to explain how it all works. Take Polygon and Circle. These geniuses are not just shapes, but entire worlds of discovery, packed with all there is to know about Line, Angle, Symmetry, Area, and more. Dive in and find out for yourself.

Line

★ Point Connector

I'm Line. No matter whether I'm a **ray** or a **line segment**, you make me every time you draw in one direction across a piece of paper. Be sure to use a ruler, though, to keep me straight as an arrow!

I may not amount to much, but none of my pals could exist without me. I form the edges of all the Geometry Genius shapes, for starters. Every time one line meets another, Angle sneaks in between them. You can measure me to find Length, who will then help you calculate Area. Wow — we're a pretty smart bunch!

- ◉ A line has only one dimension, and that is length

- ◉ Parallel lines run in the exact same direction, never touching

- ◉ Lines that meet or cross at right angles are called perpendicular

SAY WHAT?

Ray: A straight line stretching from just one point — say on another line.

Line segment: A line that stretches between two points.

✱ APPLYING SCIENCE ✱

You can use lines for all sorts of things. One clever trick is to draw a line running through the center of a shape to split it into two halves that are mirror images of each other. In such instances, the line is called a line of symmetry.

Angle

★ Turn Master

THE BIG IDEA

A measure of the space where two rays meet; measured in degrees (°). The higher the number, the bigger the angle.

If you stand still and turn to the right or left, what happens? Well, besides getting dizzy, you'll face a new direction. But did you know you're creating me — Angle?

An angle is the amount you turn through a circle. You'll find me everywhere that two lines meet. If those lines are perpendicular, I make an angle of 90° — a right angle. Any smaller than that makes an acute angle, and any bigger is obtuse, but only up to 180°. Angles with sizes of 180° to 360° are reflex. Want to get the measure of me? Use a protractor!

- We use the ° symbol — it stands for "degrees"

- A protractor is a flat tool with markings used to measure angles

- Where lines cross, their opposite angles are equal to each other

SAY WHAT?

Interior angle: The angle inside any polygon (a flat shape with straight sides), created when two lines meet each other to make the shape's sides.

APPLYING SCIENCE

All circles have 360°, so if you know one angle inside a circle (195°, for example), you can figure out how much is missing (in this case 165°). The **interior angles** of a type of shape always add up to the same number. Triangles have 180°, while quadrilaterals have 360°.

Polygon
★ Shape-Shifter

THE BIG IDEA

A shape with an inside, any number of straight sides, and a matching number of angles.

When it comes to making two-dimensional shapes, I am king! I'm not kidding! Every straight-sided shape with length (or width) and height (my two dimensions) is a polygon. Quadrilateral and Triangle? Yep, polygons. A hexagon, with six sides? A polygon, I tell you. Even million-sided megagon is one of my loyal subjects.

If my sides are all the same length, I'm "regular." But if some or all of them are different lengths, then I'm "irregular." But be careful, because shapes with curved sides don't belong in my realm — so bye-bye, Circle!

- Polygon comes from the Greek *poly* (many) and *gon* (angle)

- Polygons are named for the number of sides they have

- A polygon with ten sides is called a decagon (*deca* means ten in Greek)

SAY WHAT?

Vertex, plural vertices: The point on a polygon where two sides meet, creating an angle both inside and outside the shape.

✳ APPLYING SCIENCE ✳

Every polygon has an equal number of sides and **vertices**. So if you count the number of sides, you'll know the number of vertices as well! For example, a triangle has three sides and three vertices.

Triangle
★ Pointy Partner

THE BIG IDEA
A polygon with three sides. The angles inside a triangle always add up to 180°.

Howdy, partner! Try to find a polygon that's made *without* using me. That's right, you can't. Take any polygon you like and you'll find you can divide its shape into a number of triangles. Cool, eh?

I'm a pointy character with three straight sides, and I come in four basic types. If all of my sides are different lengths, I'm scalene. If two of my sides are the same length, I'm isosceles. If all three sides are the same length, then I'm equilateral. When two of my sides meet at a right angle, I'm a right-angled triangle.

- The *tri* in "triangle" means three in Latin
- The study of triangles is known as trigonometry
- Triangles are great for building because they're super strong

SAY WHAT?

Hypotenuse: The longest side of a right-angled triangle. It's always found opposite the right angle in the triangle.

MENTAL MATH

If you know two of the angles in a triangle, you can figure out the third. All you have to do is subtract the two you know from 180°! Try this: If one angle is 78° and another is 45°, how many degrees are in the third angle?

The answer is 57.

Quadrilateral

★ Four-sider

THE BIG IDEA

A polygon with four sides. The angles inside a quadrilateral always add up to 360°.

Dependable and true, I put the quad in *squad*ron. I'm any four-sided shape you care to think of, sharp-edged and orderly — four sides, four corners. In squares and rectangles all four corners are right angles, but not all of my regiment's shapes are so . . . well, regimented!

Take the rhombus. All sides are equal in length and opposite sides are parallel, but only opposite angles are the same. Or what about the parallelogram — an elongated rhombus, if you like, with two sets of equal (but parallel) sides. Trapezoids have one pair of parallel sides, but still count among my troops.

- All quadrilaterals are irregular, except a square, which is regular

- Some trapezoids have right angles; others are scalene or isosceles

- Squares, rectangles, and rhombuses are all parallelograms

✳ APPLYING SCIENCE ✳

Here's a quadrilateral you might know about already: a kite! It has two pairs of equal sides. Instead of being opposite each other, they are **adjacent** to one another. This makes the top part look longer or shorter than the bottom part.

Circle

★ Well-rounded Buddy

> **THE BIG IDEA**
>
> A round two-dimensional shape in which all parts of its edge are the same distance from its center.

Perfectly round and with angles adding up to 360°, I'm a real roller. You'll see my smooth shape in balls, wheels, and the sun in the sky.

Let's talk terminology! The distance from any point on my outside edge to my center is called my radius. A line passing right through my center from edge to edge is my diameter. Measure all the way around my outside edge, and you've got my circumference. You can cut me into **sectors** and **segments**. But don't confuse me with Polygon, all right? Sure, I'm two-dimensional, but I don't have any straight edges (no, thanks).

- ◉ One-quarter of a circle is known as a quadrant

- ◉ One-half of a circle is called a semicircle

SAY WHAT?

Sector: Any slice of a circle that reaches the center — for example, a slice of pizza.

Segment: Any slice of a circle that doesn't go through the center.

＊ APPLYING SCIENCE ＊

The outside edge of a circle has its own special name: circumference. It has no vertices, which is what makes circles so useful for tasks that involve spinning, rolling, and rotating.

Pi

★ Magic Constant

THE BIG IDEA

Pi is a useful mathematical **constant**: 3.14159265 . . . It is written in shorthand using the Greek letter π.

Pretty, that's me! Pretty small and pretty important! A value that never changes, I'm Pi, with a symbol that looks like this: π. It's a Greek letter, pronounced "pie." You can use me to do all kinds of clever calculations, and I'm really easy to find.

Take a circle, divide its circumference by its diameter, and there I am, always about 3.14. But there's more. Remember Square Number? Well, square Circle's radius, multiply your answer by me, and you'll have found Circle's Area. Is there no end to my magic?

⚡ SAY WHAT? ⚡

Constant: A number thought to be more interesting than others because it has uses in several different areas of mathematics.

✳ APPLYING SCIENCE ✳

Pi's digits go on forever, which means it's an irrational number! This is how it looks to the first one hundred decimal places: 3.1415926535897 93238462643383279502884 19716939937510582097 44592307816406286208 98628034825342117067 9

◉ Greek mathematician Archimedes first worked out Pi in 250 BC

◉ The world record number of digits for Pi is 31.4 trillion, set in 2019; it was discovered using Google's cloud computing service

Symmetry

★ Identical Twin

THE BIG IDEA

When a line drawn through a shape creates two identical halves, as if reflected in a mirror. It's called a **line of symmetry**.

Seeing double? Good, then you've found me: Symmetry. Pair me up with Line, and I'll turn one shape into two smaller shapes that are exactly the same as each other. Try it! Draw a diagonal line from one corner of a square to the opposite corner to make two identical triangles.

Just remember that Line has to go through a shape's center. Some shapes, such as an isosceles triangle, have just one line of symmetry. A square has four, a pentagon has five, and clever Circle has an infinite number, because you can draw a line of symmetry from anywhere on its edge!

- The simplest form of symmetry, described here, is reflection symmetry

- Sixteen capital letters are symmetrical: A, B, C, D, E, H, I, K, M, O, T, U, V, W, X, and Y.

SAY WHAT?

Line of symmetry:
A line that passes through the center of a shape, making two new congruent shapes — that is, they are the same size and the same shape.

✳ APPLYING SCIENCE ✳

Many shapes are symmetrical. A heart shape is symmetrical because it can be split in two. The same goes for a plate. But some things have no symmetry. Look at the digits from 0 to 9. Only three are perfectly symmetrical (0, 3, 8), but most are not (1, 2, 4, 5, 6, 7, 9).

2-D Shape

★ Flat Friend

THE BIG IDEA

Any shape made by drawing lines on a surface is two-dimensional.

So you've met Polygon, Triangle, Quadrilateral, and Circle. Notice something they have in common? Yep, they all appear flat when drawn on a surface. That's because they are all forms of me: 2-D Shape!

My name is short for "two-dimensional," and I'll tell you what that means. Take my pal Line. You can only measure Line along its length, so it has just one **dimension**. But look at Polygon. Sure, that shape-shifter has length (or width) too, but it also has height: two dimensions. I'm plain, but that's what makes my shapes easy to draw.

- ◉ A single point has zero dimensions

- ◉ Surfaces of walls, floors, and ceilings are all examples of 2-D shapes

- ◉ The area of math that works with 2-D shapes is plane geometry

SAY WHAT?

Dimension: A length measurement in a particular direction, such as width, height, or depth.

MATH LEGEND

Greek mathematician Euclid was one of the first people to talk about dimensions, in 300 BC. He wrote about them in a series of books called *Elements*, which were all about math. Some people say these are the most important books ever written!

3-D Shape

★ Real Rascal

THE BIG IDEA

The three dimensions that make up the world around us, forming everything you can see.

You've met my flat friend 2-D Shape, but now it's time to get real — with me, 3-D Shape! Yep, you've guessed it, my name stands for "three-dimensional." My shapes have the edge on Polygon, because they have an extra measurement: depth. Really, it is just Line heading in another direction, but it makes a huge difference.

Rather than lying flat on a surface, my shapes have **faces**, edges, and vertices. There are many different types of 3-D shapes, from spheres to cylinders, cubes, and pyramids. Even this book is 3-D, and so are you!

- Three-dimensional shapes are called "solids"

- The three dimensions are length (or width), height, and depth

- A perfect sphere is a 3-D shape with no edges

SAY WHAT?

Face: The flat surface found on any side of a 3-D shape. Each face is 2-D, but the overall shape created is 3-D.

✱ APPLYING SCIENCE ✱

A cube is a six-sided shape with square faces. A cylinder is a tube with a circle at each end. A pyramid is four triangles with a square base! And a prism has two ends that are the same, such as two congruent triangles, and sides that are rectangles.

Length

★ Distance Decider

If you've ever used a ruler to measure something in math, then you will have found me: Length. I'm the measurement that tells you the distance from one end of Line to the other. Use me to measure Polygon's sides and I'll help you find Area — just turn the page to see how.

I'm especially useful outside school. For example, I can tell you if the new couch your mom has bought will fit through the front door. And if I tell you the distance from school to home, you can figure out how long it will take to walk there!

- Measures of length include units such as feet or meters

- The Great Wall of China is a mega 13,170 miles (21,196 km) long

- The distance from Earth to the official line of space is 62 miles (100 km)

SAY WHAT?

Distance: The length between two points, like your house and the park, or even Earth and space.

✳ APPLYING SCIENCE ✳

Different countries use different systems to measure distance. In the United States, people use the U. S. Customary System, which has inches, feet, yards, and miles. Canada uses the metric system, with centimeters, meters, and kilometers.

Area

★ Space Maker

THE BIG IDEA

The size of any 2-D shape, calculated using square units, which literally means how many squares fit inside.

Picture the scene. You've used Line to draw a plan of your bedroom. Length can tell you its measurements, and these are all you need to find me — Area. I'm the amount of space contained within a shape's edges.

Say your bedroom floor is a square with sides measuring roughly 13 ft. or 4 m. Here's the math: 13 ft. × 13 ft. = 169 ft.² or 4 m × 4 m = 16 m²! Recognize my form? That's right, you already know how Square Number and Exponent work. You'll see those tiny characters in the area of any 2-D shape, as well as in the units for the area.

- ◉ Area is always measured in "square units," using the ² symbol on the unit.

- ◉ A triangle's area is half its **base** times its height

- ◉ The area of a circle is πr^2 (r stands for radius)

SAY WHAT?

Base: The edge of a 2-D shape that forms a perpendicular with the height of the shape. The base can be any one of a shape's edges.

✱ DO IT YOURSELF ✱

Imagine your bedroom is L-shaped, with a rectangle measuring roughly 6.5 ft. × 10 ft. or 2 m × 3 m, plus the original square. What's the total floor area now? You can use a calculator to figure it out.

The answer is:
65 ft.² + 169 ft.² = 234 ft.²
or 6 m² + 16 m² = 22 m²

Volume

★ Cubic Champion

☆ **THE BIG IDEA** ☆

The space inside any 3-D shape, calculated using cubic units, which literally means how many cubes fit inside.

Ha! I can only pity Area's efforts to impress. When it comes to space, I'm the real champion, because I measure 3-D shapes. I'm Volume.

Say you want to figure out the size of your lunchbox or a reading book. I work in a similar way to Area, but instead of just looking for two dimensions, you have to find all three: length (or width), height, and **depth**. Instead of ending with a square number, my answer is given as a cubic number that looks like this: ³. I've got bulk, I tell you!

SAY WHAT?

Depth: When looking at a 3-D shape, depth is the distance from the front of it to the back of it.

* **DO IT YOURSELF** *

Let's say you have a nice, regular box. It's 6 in. (15 cm) long, 4 in. (10 cm) high, and 2 in. (5 cm) deep. Can you figure out its volume? Give it a try! You might need a parent to help you . . . or a calculator!

The answer is:
6 in. × 4 in. × 2 in. = 48 in.³
(15 cm × 10 cm × 5 cm = 750 cm³)

- ◉ A three-dimensional rectangular shape is called a cuboid

- ◉ Volume can be a measure of how much sand or water fills a space

- ◉ When water freezes into ice, its volume increases!

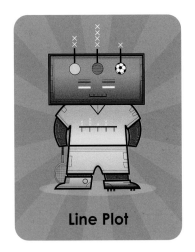

Line Plot

Bar Graph

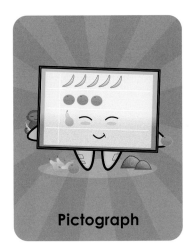

Pictograph

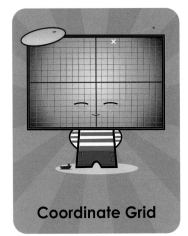

Coordinate Grid

Pie Chart

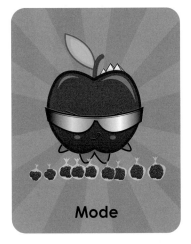

Mode

Median

Mean

Probability

Data Heroes

You know what they say, right? Always save the best for last. Well, in this math universe, that means us: the Data Heroes! We're a team of mathematical tools that help you understand the information in front of you. To make things really easy, we present data visually so that you can get a grasp of the results with one look. Oh, and did we mention we're heroes? Come and find out why.

Line Plot
★ Popularity Guru

> **THE BIG IDEA**
>
> A tally of data on a **graph** that shows the most and least popular thing in a set of data.

Running a popularity contest? Let me help. I'm Line Plot, the go-to tool for showing favorite things, such as sports, candy, and pets. I look like Number Line and run from left to right across the page.

I am so versatile — you can mark my line with numbers or with information you want to keep track of. For favorite sports, this might be football, tennis, and basketball. Above each one, in a column rising up the page, you put an x for the response of each person you ask about the sport they like best. The tallest tower of xs shows the most popular sport.

SAY WHAT?

Graph: A way of grouping data together visually so it's really easy to read.

- A line plot is a very simple type of graph
- Line plots work best with a small number of data categories to display

✻ DO IT YOURSELF ✻

Find something around your house to count. Maybe the types of shoes people wear? Count up each type and use the totals to make a line plot! Or ask your friends how many pets they have and see how that graph looks.

Bar Graph

★ Data Displayer

THE BIG IDEA

A graph that uses two **axes** and bars to display data. The bar heights help you know how much each category has.

Hi, I'm Bar Graph. I'm a little like Line Plot, but way better looking because you can color me in. I'm also more useful for dealing with bigger numbers.

Just like Line Plot, I have a line that runs from left to right across the page, marked with data groups. It's called an x-axis. But I also have a y-axis that runs vertically up the page, to make a big "L." That's where my numbers go — to show how often something occurs. But get this: I can use ones, five, tens, hundreds — you name it — which means I can handle a lot more data in one small chart.

- ● Bar graphs have spaces between the bars

- ● The highest bar shows the most popular thing in a data set

- ● You can arrange a bar graph horizontally as well as vertically

⚡ SAY WHAT? ⚡

Axis, plural axes:
A horizontal or vertical line on a graph that is labeled to show the data that has been collected.

✳ DO IT YOURSELF ✳

Try making your own bar graph. Go to your refrigerator and count the different types of food. Let's group them as meat, fruits, and vegetables. Count up how many of each there are, and then see if you can plot them on your own bar graph!

Pictograph
★ Picture Perfect

THE BIG IDEA

A graph that uses pictures to show how frequently a certain type of **data** occurs.

Bar Graph can scream and shout until it's blue in the face about being more colorful than Line Plot, but nothing beats me on looks. I'm Pictograph, and the clue to my display lies in my name . . . Bingo! I use pictures to represent data.

Say you want to count fruit in a bowl. You might draw images of apples, oranges, bananas, and pears to show exactly what's in there. Just have one image representing each piece of fruit and stack them in rows or columns. There is no end to the data that can be displayed this way.

- "Pictograph" comes from the Latin *pict,* meaning "painted"

- You can use pictures to represent a group of data

- If each picture represents a group, it is useful to include a key

SAY WHAT?

Data: Information collected about a topic so it can be analyzed or displayed.

DO IT YOURSELF

Here's a pictograph for you to make. On a trip to the zoo, you see six penguins, three lions, five elephants, and seven monkeys. Make a pretty pictograph of the different animals to keep as a reminder of your day out.

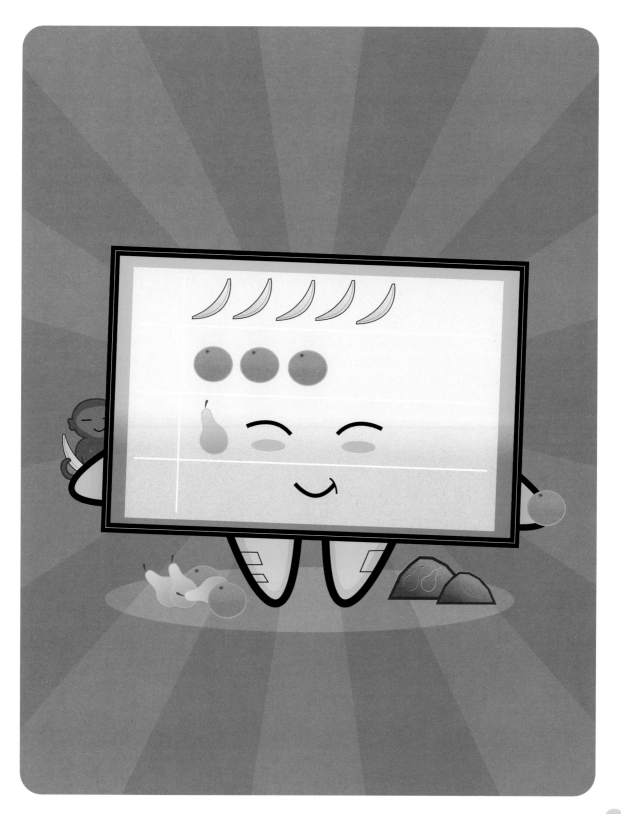

Coordinate Grid

★ Master Mapper

Looking for something? I can help! I'm Coordinate Grid, and I map out the positions of things. Like Bar Graph, I have an x-axis and a y-axis, but mine cross each other dead center. The point at which they cross is marked (0,0) and is called the origin. Numbers going up and to the right are positive. Numbers to the left and below are negative.

Coordinates come in pairs: (x, y). Say you're looking for buried treasure at (3, 7). Start at zero and take three steps along my x-axis. You'll find the treasure seven steps immediately above this, along my y-axis.

- Planes and boats use coordinates to track their location

- You can draw a line between two points to plot movement

SAY WHAT?

Coordinate: A number representing the position of something on a grid, line, or graph. Coordinates usually come in pairs.

MATH LEGEND

French mathematician René Descartes is said to have invented the coordinate system in the 1600s. He wondered how to track the position of a fly buzzing around his room. He decided coordinates would be the best system — and the rest is history.

Pie Chart
★ Wacky Wedger

☆ **THE BIG IDEA** ☆

A circle split up into sectors, with each sector showing a different set of data.

We all like pizza, so what if you want two slices, your greedy sister wants three, and your mom is happy with just one? Well, then you'd split the pizza up into two, three, and one slices. And, oops! You've accidentally made me: Pie Chart.

I show data visually, as sectors of a whole circle. I can be trickier to work with than some of the other Data Heroes, because you need to use Fraction or Decimal's **percentages** to figure out the size of my sectors. But I'm worth the effort, because I look truly fantastic once you've colored me in.

⚡ **SAY WHAT?** ⚡

Percentage: A way of showing a fraction out of 100. One percent of a pie chart is 3.6° (360 divided by 100).

✳ **APPLYING SCIENCE** ✳

Like all circles, pie charts have 360°. This is useful to know when dividing a pie chart into sectors. For the pizza above, for example, you need six sectors, each of 60° (360 ÷ 6 = 60).

- ◉ Pie charts get their name because, well, they look like pies!

- ◉ The French call them "camembert charts," after the cheese

- ◉ In Germany, they call them "cake diagrams"

Mode

★ Mostly Average

> ☆ **THE BIG IDEA** ☆
>
> The most common number in a set of numbers; the one that occurs most frequently.

You want to find the most popular number in a set of **statistics**? So use me, your good friend Mode! I make this kind of task easy.

Let's say you have some bags of apples. Each bag contains its own number of apples: 3, 4, 5, 5, 5, 6, 6, 8, 9. To find the mode, you just see which number occurs most often. In this set of numbers, you have one each of 3, 4, 8, and 9. There are two 6s and three 5s. So the answer is 5! That really is all there is to it. I am one of just three ways to find a kind of average. The other two are Median and Mean.

- Results that have two modes are called "bimodal"

- A collection of statistics about people is called a census

- Ancient Egyptians compiled the first censuses 4,000 years ago

⚡ SAY WHAT? ⚡

Statistics: A term for data that is collected and used to show trends and patterns.

✳ APPLYING SCIENCE ✳

It might surprise you, but there isn't always a simple answer for mode! If two numbers appear just as often, then you can have two modes. But if they all appear the same number of times, you can even have no mode at all.

Median

★ Middle Manager

THE BIG IDEA

The number found at the exact middle of a set of data. It gives a rough average for the whole set by dividing it exactly in half.

Sure, Mode can show you what's popular. But what if you want to find the middle value in a set of data — not what's popular, but what's "normal"? Well, hello, that's me, Median, and I'm easy to find.

How many fruits and vegetables do you normally eat? Write down your daily numbers for a week: 3, 6, 5, 4, 6, 2, 4. Some days are better than others, but what's normal? Well, write the numbers in **range** order from lowest to highest: 2, 3, 4, 4, 5, 6, 6. Find the number at the center of the line, and that's your median: 4. Not bad, but you could be eating a little better.

◉ This is a good way to find a "normal" value in a set of numbers

◉ Adding a new data value changes the position of the median number

◉ With even data, the median falls halfway between two data points

SAY WHAT?

Range: The difference between the lowest number and the highest number in a set of data.

MENTAL MATH

A student has their test scores. They got an 87 on the first test, then 77, 79, 91, 82, 85, and 78. They need a median of 80 to pass. Can you figure out whether or not they succeeded?

The answer is yes! The range goes 77, 78, 79, 82, 85, 87, 91, and the median is 82.

Mean

★ Truly Average

> **THE BIG IDEA**
> The mathematical average of a data set, calculated by adding all the values in the set and dividing by the number of values.

Mean, Median, and Mode: the three amigos! I'm Mean, and some say I'm the most useful. I agree . . . is that so very *mean* of me? I am the true average for any of list of values. Try me out!

Playing card games with your pal, you win some and you lose some, but how do you do on average? The last eight days you've played, you've won the following number of games out of ten: 3, 6, 9, 6, 5, 7, 4, 8. Just add up all your wins and divide the answer by the number of days you have played: 48 ÷ 8 = 6. Well done, that's a good average!

- Results can be **skewed** by a really big or small number in the set

- Averages are used in sports statistics to help compare athletes

> ⚡ **SAY WHAT?** ⚡
>
> **Skewed:** In averages, skewed results are distorted in a way that is seen as inaccurate or misleading.

> ✳ **MENTAL MATH** ✳
>
> Try this list of numbers: 1, 2, 2, 4, 6, 9, 11, 13, 15. Now, can you figure out the mean for them? Have a go!
>
> The answer is 7. The total comes to 63, and there are 9 numbers: 63 ÷ 9 = 7.

Probability

★ The Chance Taker

THE BIG IDEA

The **chance** of something happening in a given situation. Probabilities are expressed as percents from 0% to 100%.

Perhaps there was a 40 percent chance of rain today. That's me: Probability! I'm a way of saying how likely something is to happen. I say it's 100% probable when an event is guaranteed to happen (like you going to bed tonight), but it's 0% probable when an event is impossible.

Say you have three yellow balls in a box of 30 colored balls. How likely are you to pick a yellow ball without looking? I divide the number of yellow balls by the total number of balls ($3 \div 30 = 0.1$). Then I multiply the answer by 100: 10. So there is a 10 percent chance.

- Probability can be presented as a fraction: $\frac{1}{2}$ is a 50% chance

- Percentages are expressed using a symbol that looks like this: %

- A six-sided die has six equally likely outcomes, each with a $\frac{1}{6}$ chance

SAY WHAT?

Chance: This is the likelihood of something happening. It is often rated on a scale of 0 to 1, or 0 to 100 if using percentages.

MENTAL MATH

Imagine you have 50 balls: 20 red, 20 blue, and 10 yellow. What's the chance of picking a yellow one now?

Well, $10 \div 50$ is $\frac{1}{5}$, which is also 0.2. Multiplied by 100 gives a 20 percent chance!

Glossary

Adjacent: Close to or near something. In geometry, adjacent sides are next to each other — they touch at one end.

Algebra: Mathematics that uses letters and symbols to represent numbers and form equations.

Axis, plural axes: A horizontal or vertical line on a graph that is labeled to show the data that has been collected.

Base: The edge of a 2-D shape that forms a perpendicular with the height of the shape. It can be any one of a shape's edges.

Chance: The possibility or likelihood of something happening, often rated on a scale of 0 to 1, or 0 to 100 if using percentages.

Constant: A number thought to be more interesting than others because it has uses in several different areas of mathematics.

Coordinate: A number representing the position of something on a grid, line, or graph. Coordinates usually come in pairs.

Data: Information collected about a topic so it can be analyzed or displayed.

Decimal point: A point placed after a number, where anything to the right of the point is a fraction of the whole number to the left.

Denominator: The bottom number in a fraction; it tells you how many parts make the whole.

Depth: When looking at a 3-D shape, depth is the distance from the front of it to the back of it.

Difference: The term used to describe the answer to a subtraction problem.

Digit: Any whole number from zero to nine. All large numbers are made up of digits.

Dimension: A length measurement in a particular direction, such as width, height, or depth.

Distance: The length between two points, such as your house and the park, or Earth and space.

Divisor: The name given to the number doing the dividing. In 20 ÷ 5, the divisor is 5.

Equals sign: This symbol (=) works like a balance — an expression or number on one side equals that on the other side: 4 × 3 = 20 − 8

Equation: A math statement in which elements on either side of an equal sign are the same. For example, 1 + 2 = 3.

Factor: Factors are numbers you can multiply together to get another number.

Graph: A way of grouping data together visually so it's really easy to read.

Hypotenuse: The longest side of a right-angled triangle. It's always found opposite the right angle in the triangle.

Interior angle: The angle inside any polygon, created when two lines meet each other to make the shape's sides.

Irrational number: Decimal numbers that never end and do not repeat are called irrational numbers.

Lemniscate: The name given to infinity's "sideways eight" looped symbol (∞).

Line segment: A line that stretches between two points.

Line of symmetry: A line that passes through the center of a shape, making two new congruent shapes — that is, they are the same size and the same shape.

Metric system: A system of units that uses things in multiples of ten, such as centimeters, meters, and kilometers.

Multiplication: Lists that show the numbers 1 to 12 multiplied by each other. They are handy for finding products quickly.

Natural numbers: Also called counting numbers, these are any whole numbers above (but not including) zero.

Negative: Any number below zero is negative. A negative number is written using a negative sign: –5. A number above zero is positive.

Not-whole number: Any number that has a fraction with it, or that has numbers after its decimal point.

Numerator: The top number in a fraction; it tells you how many parts of the whole you have.

Operation: One of four major processes used in math: addition, subtraction, multiplication, and division.

Parallel: When two lines run alongside each other, always the same distance apart and never touching.

Percentage: A way of showing a fraction out of 100. One percent of a pie chart is 3.6° (360 divided by 100).

Perpendicular: Two lines that pass over each other to make the shape of a cross and forming right angles where they meet (90°).

Product: The name given to the result when you multiply numbers together: 10 is the product of 2 × 5.

Quotient: The resulting number when you divide one number by another.

Radix point: A symbol that is used to separate a whole number from its fractions — more commonly called "decimal point."

Ray: A straight line stretching from just one point — say, on another line.

Remainder: Anything that's left over as a fraction after dividing two numbers together.

Sector: Any slice of a circle that reaches the center — a slice of pizza, for example.

Segment: Any slice of a circle that doesn't go through the center.

Skewed: In averages, skewed results are distorted in a way that is seen as inaccurate or misleading.

Square root: The number used to make a square number. For example, 5 is the square root of 25, because 5 × 5 = 25.

Statistics: A term for data that is collected and used to show trends and patterns.

Sum: Adding any two or more numbers together is called finding a sum: 1 plus 1 creates a sum, and so does 2 plus 5 plus 3 plus 1.

Tally: A score of how often something occurs or happens.

Unit: A single group of something. Unit can also mean "1."

U.S. Customary System: A system of units that includes such things as inches, feet, miles, and gallons.

Vertex, plural vertices: The point on a polygon where two sides meet, creating an angle both inside and outside the shape.

Index